WE GO ECO

THE ANIMALS WE SAVE

WRITTEN BY KATIE WOOLLEY

ILLUSTRATED BY SOPHIE FOSTER

WINDMILL BOOKS

Published in 2027 by Windmill Books,
an Imprint of Rosen Publishing
2544 Clinton St.
Buffalo, NY 14224

First published in Great Britain in 2023 by Hodder and Stoughton

Illustrators: Sophie Foster and Hannah Wood
Designer: Lisa Peacock
In-House Editor: Melanie Palmer

Picture credits:
p29 Frank Micelotta/PictureGroup for National Geographic/Shutterstock

Cataloging-in-Publication Data
Names: Woolley, Katie, author. | Foster, Sophie, illustrator.
Title: The animals we save / by Katie Woolley, illustrated by Sophie Foster.
Description: Buffalo, NY : Windmill Books, an imprint of Rosen Publishing, 2027. |
Series: We go eco | Includes glossary and index.
Identifiers: ISBN 9781725398511 (pbk.) | ISBN 9781725398528 (library bound) | ISBN 9781725398535 (ebook)
Subjects: LCSH: Animals--Juvenile literature. | Biodiversity conservation--Juvenile literature. |
Wildlife conservation--Juvenile literature.
Classification: LCC QL49.W66 2027 | DDC 590--dc23

Printed in China

CPSIA Compliance Information: Batch #QS27WM
For Further Information contact Rosen Publishing at 1-800-237-9932

CONTENTS

ANIMALS ON EARTH

Earth is home to millions of animals. They have adapted to survive on every continent and in many different habitats, from oceans and rivers to deserts and jungles.

Earth is connected by different habitats. Plants, animals, and people share these places, living side by side.

mammals

reptiles

fish

amphibians

bugs

CLIMATE CHANGE

Animals also share Earth with people. But people have not always taken very good care of the planet. Our actions have led to global warming and climate change.

Climate change is causing Earth's temperature to rise, making it hard for some animals to survive.

Polar ice is melting earlier and earlier each year. Polar bears must swim further to hunt and reach land.

Oceans are filling up with people's plastic waste. Rainforests are being cut down to make room for more homes.

As the number of people on Earth grows, the amount of waste people throw away will grow.

OCEAN ANIMALS

Earth's water is in the clouds, in the rivers and streams, in the polar ice, and in the oceans. But people's actions are harming our oceans.

A quarter of all sea animals live in or near coral reefs.

As Earth gets hotter, sea water gets warmer, too. This temperature rise can cause some coral reefs to die.

Turtles lay their eggs on beaches. As Earth's temperature rises, sand gets warmer, too. Warmer sand means more female turtles hatch than male ones.

Not enough male turtles could mean the species becomes extinct.

Eco-Tip
Make a poster to tell people about coral reefs and climate change.

THE FUTURE OF OCEANS

People throw away a lot of plastic every day. Some of this trash ends up in the ocean. Sea animals can't always tell the difference between plastic and food. Some turtles have eaten plastic bags because they look like jellyfish.

The Great Pacific Garbage Patch is an area of trash three times bigger than France!

Eco-Tip
Throw your trash out after a day at the beach.

In Sydney, Australia, two people came up with the Seabin. It's a trash can in the water that can collect trash, oil, and chemicals.

There are over 800 Seabins around the world.

DESERT AND GRASSLAND ANIMALS

Deserts are huge habitats that don't get a lot of rain. As Earth gets hotter and less rain falls, droughts mean more land becomes a desert. This is called desertification.

Deserts are found on every continent. Antarctica is a cold desert.

Eco-Tip

Do not waste water at home. Turn off the faucet when you are brushing your teeth to save water.

Grasslands are meadows, savannas, and other habitats where some rain falls, but not enough for forests to grow. More and more people are taking over these areas of grassland to farm. This means there is less room for animals.

Grasslands are home to zebras, antelope, and other animals, including those shown here.

THE FUTURE OF DESERTS AND GRASSLANDS

We need to protect deserts and grasslands. When we take over land, people and animals are forced to live closer together. In some parts of the world, people have to share their land with big, wild animals.

When elephants come across farm crops, they want to eat them. Farmers try to scare the animals away with loud noises, traps, and even fires.

In Tanzania, cloth covered in chili oil is tied to fences to keep the elephants away from farmers' crops. The fences are cheap and easy to make. This keeps farmers happy and elephants safe.

JUNGLE AND RAINFOREST ANIMALS

Jungles and rainforests are home to over three-quarters of all life on land. We need to protect these habitats for all animals.

Eco-Tip
Use less paper to save more trees by writing on both sides and recycling it if you can.

- Predators, such as leopards, live and rest in the trees.
- Monkey troops swing from branch to branch.

- Reptiles, such as snakes, hunt in the trees.

- Unusual species live nowhere else on Earth.

- Birds, insects, and small mammals find food on the jungle floor.

As Earth gets hotter and less rain arrives during the dry months, more wildfires happen. These fires destroy parts of forests, harming animals.

THE FUTURE OF JUNGLES AND FORESTS

People cut down rainforest trees to make room for farmland and homes. Every minute, an area of the Amazon rainforest the size of a soccer field is cut down. This is called deforestation.

These monkeys are also hunted for food.

Black spider monkeys live high up in the rainforests of Central and South America. They need the jungle treetops to be close together to move through the forest.

When people cut down jungle trees, they harm animals such as black spider monkeys. People sell the monkeys illegally as pets.

Rangers now patrol the forest in Central America, protecting the monkeys and the trees!

ECO-TIP

Look at the labels on your food. Find out which foods have been grown or made in rainforests.

POLAR ANIMALS

The Arctic and Antarctica are harsh frozen places that are still full of life.

As Earth's temperature rises, ice melts at a faster rate every year. This has a huge impact on the wildlife in these habitats.

- Walruses need the sea ice to rest and feed.

ECO-TIP

The energy we use plays a part in climate change. We all need to use less energy to help protect polar animals.

- Reindeer have been forced to migrate earlier in the year when the young reindeer aren't strong enough.

- Less sea ice means that some whales, like narwhals, have fewer places to hide from predators.

- Warmer seas and melting sea ice has led to less krill for large animals, such as the big humpback whale.

THE FUTURE OF THE POLAR ICE CAPS

People are working hard to protect the animals that live in the Arctic and Antarctica. Scientists have spent many years finding out how some animals are coping with climate change.

Polar bears need sea ice for traveling, hunting, resting, and raising their babies.

Sea ice reflects the sun's heat. This helps keep Earth cool. But as more ice melts, the future of these habitats is uncertain.

The Arctic Ice Project wants to stop this ice from melting by scattering a layer of glass powder across the ice. The glass will reflect more of the sun's rays and help keep the ice frozen.

WHAT CAN WE DO AT HOME?

You can help wildlife all around the world by doing things to reduce climate change.

- At home, leave out food and water for local birds and bees.

- Stay on paths and do not disturb habitats when you are out and about.

- Recycle plastic or reuse it in craft projects.

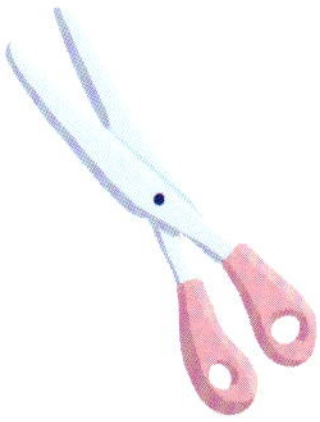

- Take part in a trash collecting event on your street or at a local park.

- Be a nature spotter! Record the birds you see, and ask an adult to help you share the information.

BECOME AN ECO WARRIOR

Talk about climate change with your friends and family. Tell them about some of the animals in danger because of people's actions.

- Make posters that show people how Earth's animals are in danger.

Eco-Tip
Hold a secondhand clothes sale or bake sale at school to raise money for a wildlife charity.

Find out about rewilding – the return of habitats to their wild state. For example, beavers have been reintroduced in Scotland. By gnawing wood, they provide homes for other animals, and their dams can help control the flow of river water.

EARTH ACTIVIST: TXAI SURUÍ

Txai Suruí was born in Brazil to an Indigenous people called the Suruí. She set up the Movement of the Indigenous Youth of Rondônia. She fights to protect the land, the people, and the wildlife that live in her local area. She raises awareness of deforestation and the harm it causes to Indigenous people who live in the forests.

Visit your local library or look online to find out more about the lives of Indigenous people.

GLOSSARY

Adapts when a species becomes better-suited to their home

Climate change the long-term changes in Earth's temperature often caused by people

Continent a large area of land; there are seven continents on Earth

Deforestation when trees are cut down to clear the land and make room for other uses, such as farmland

Desertification the process of land turning into desert

Drought no rain over a long time

Extinct the dying out of a species

Global warming the rising of the average temperature on Earth

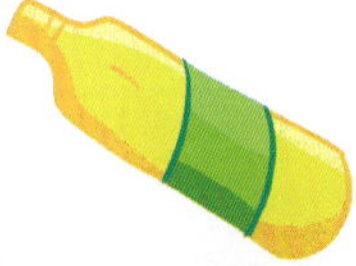

Grassland a big area with low-growing plants, such as grass

Habitat the usual place where a living thing lives

Invent to make something for the first time

Krill small, shrimp-like animals that live in the ocean

Migrate take a long journey to a new home, often moving between summer and winter homes

Protect look after and care for something

Rainforest an area of forest that gets a lot of rain

Species a group of similar living things

Survive remain alive

Wildfire an uncontrolled fire that burns in a forest or grassland

INDEX